MUHAMMAD ALI

GREAT LIVES IN GRAPHICS

Button
BOOKS

Muhammad Ali was one of the greatest boxers and sports personalities of all time. An Olympic gold medallist and three-time world heavyweight champion, his prowess in the ring and showmanship outside of it made him the most famous fighter who ever lived. Some of his fights are among the most-watched sports events ever broadcast, including the legendary 'Rumble in the Jungle' and 'Thrilla in Manila' matches.

Aside from his athletic career, Ali was a minister in the Nation of Islam and an ambassador for humanitarian causes. In his personal life, Ali became known for standing up for his religious and political beliefs even when they were unpopular, helping to educate millions of people about the racial prejudice faced by Black Americans and the injustices of the Vietnam War. Let's meet this sporting icon…

ALI'S WORLD

1960
Ali wins a gold medal at the Summer Olympics in Italy.

1961
John F Kennedy becomes President of the United States.

1942
Muhammad Ali is born on 17 January in Louisville, Kentucky, US.

1958
Start of the Pizza Hut restaurant chain.

1964
Ali becomes heavyweight champion of the world for the first time.

1945
World War II ends.

1947
Pilot Chuck Yeager breaks the sound barrier in the Bell X-1 aircraft.

1967
Ali refuses to fight in the Vietnam War and receives a five-year prison sentence.

1954
Start of the Vietnam War.

1952
Elizabeth II becomes Queen of the United Kingdom.

1969
The Apollo 11 astronauts land on the Moon.

1982
Michael Jackson's *Thriller* is released and becomes the best-selling album of all time.

2000
The International Space Station becomes operational.

2002
The Euro currency enters circulation.

1984
Ali is diagnosed with Parkinson's disease.

1996
Ali carries the Olympic torch at the Summer Games in Atlanta, US.

1978
Ali becomes the first person to win the world heavyweight title three times.

2008
Barack Obama becomes the first Black President of the United States.

1974
Ali defeats George Foreman in the famous 'Rumble in the Jungle' fight and becomes heavyweight champion again.

1995
The first computer-animated film, *Toy Story*, is released.

1986
The Chernobyl nuclear disaster in Ukraine.

1991
Collapse of the Soviet Union.

2012
Summer Olympics held in London for the third time.

1972
The early arcade game Pong is released.

1989
British scientist Tim Berners-Lee invents the World Wide Web.

R.I.P.

2016
Muhammad Ali dies on 3 June in Scottsdale, Arizona.

HARD KNOCK LIFE

Muhammad Ali, birth name Cassius Marcellus Clay Jr, was born in Louisville in the south-eastern state of Kentucky in the US in 1942. During his childhood years, racial discrimination against Black Americans was still widespread in the south. His experiences of racism shaped the political and personal choices he made in later life

THE CLAY FAMILY

Clay grew up in a **poor household**. His father made a living by painting billboards and signs, while his mother worked as a **maid**. His life was similar to that of the many other **struggling Black families** in the south at the time.

SCHOOL

WHITE ENTRANCE

COLORED ENTRANCE

SEGREGATION

Separating one group of people from another

The name **JIM CROW** came from an offensive term used to refer to Black people

'JIM CROW'

Although slavery was abolished in the US in 1865, **prejudice against Black people continued**. In the southern states after the American Civil War and into the early 20th century, a series of laws were introduced that segregated the black and white populations. These became known as the **Jim Crow laws.** The laws stated that Black people would be treated as 'separate, but equal', yet in reality the facilities, jobs and homes available to them were much worse.

WHITE   COLORED

VOTE

There were segregated:
NEIGHBOURHOODS
SCHOOLS
RESTAURANTS
THEATRES
HOSPITALS
WAITING ROOMS
PUBLIC BATHROOMS
WATER FOUNTAINS
CEMETERIES

Black people faced unfair treatment in every area of life, including:
LOWER PAY
VOTING RIGHTS REMOVED
LONGER JAIL SENTENCES

MARRIAGE BETWEEN A WHITE PERSON AND A BLACK PERSON WAS ILLEGAL IN KENTUCKY AND COULD BE PUNISHED BY IMPRISONMENT.

KENTUCKY

SOUTHERN STATES

THE GREAT MIGRATION

Tired of their constant mistreatment, many educated Black people **moved north** from the southern states from the 1920s into the 1970s in search of a **better life**. Sadly, they discovered that there was almost as much discrimination where they arrived. In the 1940s in the north, there were still businesses that would only serve white people and areas where Black people were not allowed to live.

THE KU KLUX KLAN

White hatred and hostility towards Black people even turned violent. A racist secret organisation known as the Ku Klux Klan, started in 1865, carried out **acts of terror** against Black people, including destroying their schools and churches and even **murdering** some Black citizens.

TIME FOR CHANGE

The misery and oppression of the Jim Crow era led Black people to organise and push for greater freedom and equality. This became the **Civil Rights movement** of the 1950s and 60s.

LEARNING THE ROPES

Believe it or not, it was a stolen bike that led to Clay's boxing career! Aged 12, he told a Louisville police officer called Joe Martin that he wanted to beat up the thief who'd taken his bicycle. Martin, who also trained young boxers at a gym, told Clay that he'd have to learn to fight first! Clay started taking lessons from Martin and soon showed great promise, but his unconventional style and flamboyant behaviour angered many old-school purists...

YOUNG CASSIUS

CLAY'S KILLER MOVES:
* FAST FOOT SPEED
* QUICK AND POWERFUL JABS

WIN!

Aged 12
Clay wins his first amateur match by split decision: when two of the three judges score in favour of the winner.

WIN!

Aged 14
Clay wins the Golden Gloves tournament for new boxers in the light heavyweight class. What's next?

WIN!

Aged 17
Clay wins the National Golden Gloves Tournament of Champions and the Amateur Athletic Union's national title.

WIN!

Aged 18
Clay begins a professional career. He wins his debut fight on the 29 October 1960.

FIGHTING TALK!

To increase public interest in his fights, Clay became known for reciting his own poetry and humorous, memorable phrases, including describing himself as 'the greatest'. He gained a reputation as a charming and colourful personality in and out of the ring.

NEVER PUT YOUR MONEY AGAINST CASSIUS CLAY, FOR YOU WILL NEVER HAVE A LUCKY DAY.

EVERYONE KNEW WHEN I STEPPED IN TOWN, I WAS THE GREATEST FIGHTER AROUND.

FLOAT LIKE A BUTTERFLY, STING LIKE A BEE!

How Clay described his boxing style

'LOUISVILLE LIP': the nickname Clay was given because of his bragging.

Clay's fighting style was different to the norm. He would:

- Back away from punches, instead of bobbing and weaving to avoid hits
- Hold his hands lower than other fighters

1.91M CLAY'S HEIGHT

PUNCH PROPHECIES

Another element of Clay's showmanship was his habit of predicting in which round he'd knock out an opponent before a fight!

RUMBLE RECORD

WON ALL 19

OF FIRST PROFESSIONAL FIGHTS, INCLUDING

15 KNOCKOUTS

Game on

There's a lot more to boxing than simply hitting the other person as hard as you can. If you want to be a winner, you need to learn the strategies for success and keep within the rules…

The aim of the game

Putting it bluntly, knocking out your opponent or beating them so badly that they decide to give up before the match is over (this is called a technical knockout)!

SCORING

If you can't win by knockout, it's up to the three ringside judges to decide who's the victor. After the 12 rounds, each judge reaches their own conclusion about which fighter gave the best performance.

SPLIT DECISION: 2 out of 3 judges vote in favour of one fighter

UNANIMOUS DECISION: all 3 judges vote in favour of one fighter

DRAW: 2 out of 3 judges mark the fighters equal, or 1 judge marks them equal and the other 2 judges are split

12 rounds

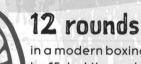

in a modern boxing match. There used to be 15, but it was dropped to 12 after the tragic death of South Korean boxer Kim Duk-koo in the 14th round of a title fight against Ray Mancini in 1982.

EACH ROUND LASTS 3 MINUTES WITH 1 MINUTE REST IN BETWEEN EACH ROUND

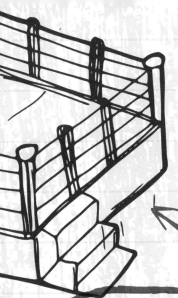

The referee

He stays in the ring with the boxers and regulates the match, making sure the rules are followed.

5.5 to 6.7 metres
Size of the boxing ring

Some rules of fighting

1 Only allowed to punch your opponent with a clenched fist.

2 Any strike must be above the opponent's belt and not in their kidneys, neck or the back of their head.

3 You can't hit an opponent who's down on the ground.

4 You can't use the ropes to gain leverage.

There is no universally accepted body that enforces the rules of boxing and each country has their own variations.

'Punch drunk'

Unsurprisingly, boxing can be a dangerous sport. A professional career in boxing comes with the risk of serious injury or even death. Chronic encephalopathy, or dementia pugilistica (often called being 'punch drunk' by boxers) is a degenerative brain disease that can affect boxers and other people who have suffered repetitive head injuries. The symptoms include:

HEADACHE | DEPRESSION | AGGRESSION

SHORT-TERM MEMORY LOSS | DEMENTIA-LIKE DECLINE IN MENTAL ABILITIES

MARQUESS OF QUEENSBERRY RULES

This code of rules written by a member of the British Amateur Athletic Club was published in 1867 and is one of the biggest influences on the rules of modern boxing.
The Queensberry rules include:

* NO WRESTLING OR HUGGING ALLOWED

* A MAN HANGING ON THE ROPES IN A HELPLESS STATE, WITH HIS TOES OFF THE GROUND, SHALL BE CONSIDERED DOWN

* NO SHOES OR BOOTS WITH SPRINGS ALLOWED

READY TO RUMBLE

Boxing is one of the oldest sports in the world. It's not very surprising, since all you need to play is two pairs of fists! What is its history and how has it changed over the centuries?

First known boxing rules from ancient Greece

1. THE FIGHT CONTINUES UNTIL ONE MAN HOLDS UP A FINGER TO SIGNAL DEFEAT OR IS PHYSICALLY UNABLE TO CONTINUE

2. HOLDING AN OPPONENT CLOSE WITH ONE OR BOTH ARMS IS STRICTLY FORBIDDEN

3. CONTESTS HELD OUTDOORS IN THE HEAT AND BRIGHT SUNLIGHT

BRUTAL BRAWLING

In ancient Rome, boxers would wear gloves with **spikes and lumps of metal** sewn into the leather. Ouch! In gladiatorial boxing, the match usually wouldn't end until one fighter lay dead.

3000-1350BC

Bare-fisted boxers and spectators are shown in ancient **Sumerian** and **Egyptian relief carvings.**

1500BC

Earliest image of boxers wearing hand coverings, on a carved vase from the **Minoan civilisation** in Crete, Greece.

'A BOXER'S VICTORY IS GAINED IN BLOOD'

1ST CENTURY BC GREEK INSCRIPTION

PUGILISM

Another name for boxing, which comes from the Latin word pugil meaning 'boxer'.

1719

One of the earliest boxing celebrities, **James Figg,** is named 'champion of England' and keeps the title for 15 years.

BARE-KNUCKLE BRITAIN

Boxing became popular again in 17th-century Britain, where fighters would compete for prize money. There were almost no rules: matches were fought gloveless, there were no weight divisions saving smaller men from having to fight much bigger ones, and wrestling was allowed! The sport was illegal, but very popular with the public.

WHEN IT COMES TO FIGHTING, I'M 'ARMLESS

19TH CENTURY

During the **Victorian era,** a time when society in Britain became more morally conservative, **boxing declined** in popularity because it was seen as uncivilised. Meanwhile, its popularity increased in the United States where it was seen as a route to fame and wealth.

18TH CENTURY

Mufflers, the precursor to modern boxing gloves, are introduced. Many believe that it's actually the introduction of gloves that made boxing more dangerous. During the days of bare-knuckle fighting, opponents would typically aim for the body, but once gloves started being worn they would usually aim for the head, which made brain damage much more likely.

WWI
(1914-1918)

Boxing is used as a training tool by the **American Army** to prepare soldiers for combat.

GOING FOR GOLD

Just before he began his professional career, Clay was selected for the US's Olympic boxing team for the 1960 Summer Olympics in Rome, Italy. His lightning-fast reflexes and pulverising punches led to a gold medal and his first taste of international fame

PANCRATIUM

This brutal event was a bit like boxing, wrestling and street fighting all rolled into one. The contestants could kick and hit an opponent on the ground - only biting and eye-gouging were banned! Unsurprisingly, pancratium is not part of the modern games.

WHAT ARE THE OLYMPIC GAMES?

This sports festival traces its history back over 2,000 years to ancient Greece, where amateur athletes would compete in a series of events. The original games were held every four years and were an important part of the religious life of the Greeks, held in honour of the god Zeus. Some of the early events included a footrace, discus throwing, wrestling, the long jump – and boxing.

BLAST FROM THE PAST

The Olympic Games were revived in the late 19th century. Originally, the games were only open to amateurs, but since the 1980s professionals have been allowed to compete in many events. There are summer and winter games, both taking place every four years, featuring a wide range of sports.

In most events, the contestants took part naked!

4 Clay won all four of his Olympic fights. He beat Zbigniew Pietrzykowski of Poland in the final to win the light heavyweight Olympic gold medal.

POLISH PROWESS

Pietrzykowski is Poland's most famous boxer. He won one silver and two bronze medals at the Olympic Games between 1956 and 1964, as well as four gold medals at the European Championships. After his boxing career ended, he became a trainer and served as vice-chairman of the Sports Committee as a member of the Polish Parliament.

PASSING THE TORCH

Long after his boxing career had ended, Clay was invited back to the Olympics to light the torch during the opening ceremony of the 1996 Games in Atlanta, US.

1896 FIRST MODERN OLYMPIC GAMES

LONDON IS THE ONLY CITY TO HOST THE SUMMER GAMES 3 TIMES

29 NUMBER OF SUMMER OLYMPICS HELD SO FAR

3

21 HOW MANY CITIES HAVE HOSTED THE SUMMER OLYMPICS

3.6BN HOW MANY PEOPLE WATCHED CLAY LIGHT THE TORCH. AT THE TIME, IT WAS THE MOST WATCHED TELEVISED EVENT IN HISTORY!

BLOW-BY-BLOW

On 25 February, 1964, Clay got his first shot at the title of heavyweight champion of the world against the reigning number one, Sonny Liston. Clay won a surprise victory that catapulted him to stardom and set him on the path of becoming one of the 20th century's greatest athletes.

SONNY LISTON

HEAVYWEIGHT CHAMPION 1962-1964

1.85M TALL

SON OF A FARMER

50 WINS INCLUDING 39 BY KNOCKOUTS

SKILLS: POWERFUL PUNCHES, ENDURANCE AND STAMINA

SAID TO HAVE LEARNED BOXING WHILE SERVING TWO LONG PRISON SENTENCES

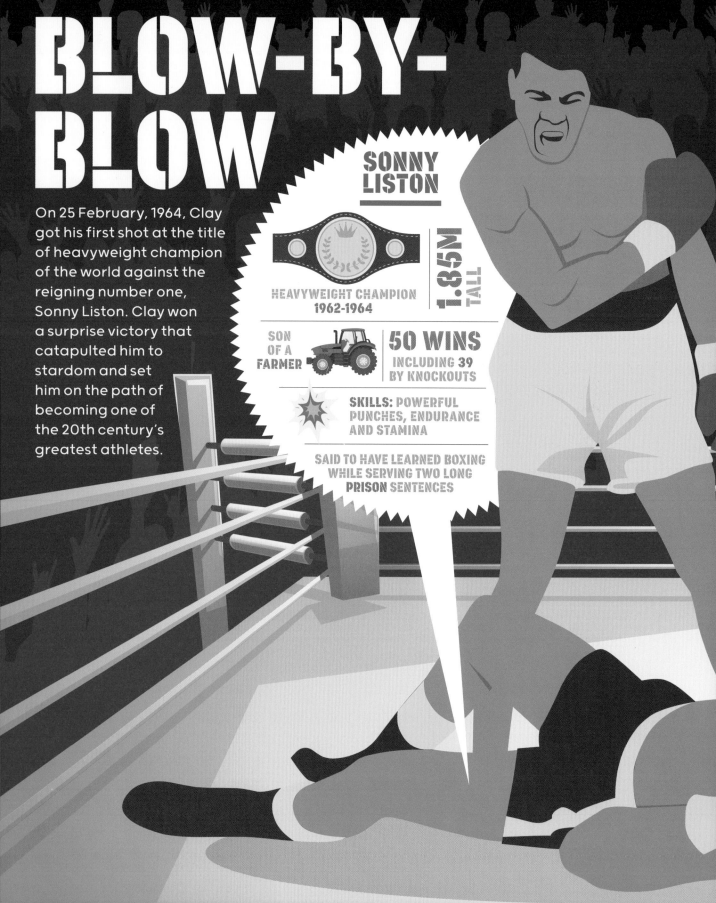

THROWING IN THE TOWEL

Liston, known at the time as one of the most fearsome and powerful boxers in the world, barely bothered to train for his fight with Clay, believing that he didn't pose a threat. In the ring, it was a different story. Clay showed that he was no pushover, and at the end of the sixth round Liston refused to go on, citing a shoulder injury as the reason. Clay was declared the new heavyweight champion.

'Yes, the crowd did not dream when they lay down their money

That they would see a total eclipse of the Sonny.' ←

Part of Clay's poem before the title fight

REMATCH

On 25 May, 1965, Clay and Liston met again. In another shock result, Clay knocked out Liston in the first round. The fight remains one of the most controversial boxing matches ever. It is known that Liston was involved with organised crime figures in the boxing world, and some have claimed that he fixed the fight, losing on purpose.

'THE PHANTOM PUNCH'

This is how the blow that Clay landed on Liston that ended the fight has been described. Some witnesses claimed that the punch didn't connect with Liston's head and that his KO was staged.

SONNY'S MYSTERIOUS LIFE... AND DEATH

Sonny Liston's life was shrouded in mystery. Born into poverty in a shack outside Forrest City in Arkansas, he suffered **repeated beatings** at the hands of his abusive father. He claimed not to know exactly how old he was. Unable to read or write, he turned to **armed robbery** to make a living and was constantly in trouble with the law. Eventually he found success by channelling his energies and ambitions into boxing. He was found dead in his home in Las Vegas in 1971 – some believe that he was **murdered by the mob.**

FINDING RELIGION

He was born Cassius Clay, but he became Muhammad Ali. How? Ali's transformation is down to his involvement with the Nation of Islam from 1964…

6 March, 1964
Clay takes the new name of Muhammad Ali, chosen for him by his spiritual mentor, Elijah Muhammad, the leader of the Nation of Islam.

WHAT IS THE NATION OF ISLAM?

A movement founded by and for **Black Americans** in the 19th century that combined beliefs from the religion of Islam with Black nationalist ideas. Many African slaves brought to America had been Muslims, so the movement was an attempt to **reconnect** modern Black Americans with their history and rich culture.

A NEW NATION?

Converts to the Nation of Islam thought that Black Americans should seek economic independence from the white majority. Some even argued for a separate Black nation in Georgia, Alabama and Mississippi.

USA

MISSISSIPPI

GEORGIA

ALABAMA

BELIEFS & RULES

SUBMISSION TO ALLAH (GOD)

IMPORTANCE OF A STRONG FAMILY LIFE

NO SMOKING, DRINKING ALCOHOL OR TAKING DRUGS

NO EATING PORK

GOING MAINSTREAM

The movement gained a much higher profile in the 1950s when the charismatic leader Malcolm Little – or **Malcolm X** – took over the Nation of Islam's **New York Temple.**

MALCOLM X 1925-1965

 Academically gifted at school, but prejudice against Black students made him lose interest in studying.

 Turned to petty crime as a young man and was imprisoned.

 Converted to Nation of Islam in jail and became one of its most famous and controversial spokespersons.

Later converted to orthodox Islam and distanced himself from the more extreme, separatist views of Nation of Islam leader Elijah Muhammad.

 Assassinated by a Nation of Islam member in 1965.

An iconic figure of the Civil Rights era in American history.

1970s

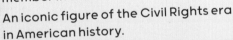

Ali studies the **Quran**, the Islamic holy book, and **converts** to orthodox Islam.

X MARKS THE SPOT

Members of the Nation of Islam would take a new Muslim name or use an 'X' in place of their birth name to show that their original African names had been taken from them when their ancestors were enslaved.

WHAT WAS THE VIETNAM WAR?

A long and bloody war, with the Communist government of North Vietnam and its supporters in South Vietnam on one side, and the South Vietnamese government and its allies, especially the United States, on the other. The conflict was part of the larger Cold War between the United States and the Soviet Union.

WHAT HAPPENED TO ALI?

'I AIN'T GOT NO QUARREL WITH THEM V'

THE VIETCONG WERE THE GUERRILLA FIGHTERS SUPPORTING THE NORTH VIETNAMESE ARMY AGAINST THE US FORCES.

1954-1975
DATES OF THE VIETNAM WAR

SEEN AS A 'DRAFT DODGER' BY THE PUBLIC

STRIPPED OF HIS HEAVYWEIGHT TITLE

BOXING LICENCE SUSPENDED, MEANING HE COULDN'T FIGHT

TURNING THE TIDE

Ali spent the time away from boxing talking on college campuses about why he refused to fight in Vietnam. Eventually, public opinion started to shift in his favour, as the war dragged on and more and more American soldiers were killed in battle.

NO MORE

STOP THE WAR

1970
ALI'S BOXING LICENCE IS RESTORED

1971
HIS CONVICTION IS OVERTURNED BY THE US SUPREME COURT

US

Public opinion suddenly turned against Ali when, in 1967, he refused to be drafted into the US army during the Vietnam War. He gave his religious beliefs and the fact that he was a Muslim minister as the reason. He said that he was not willing to fight for a government and a country that had oppressed his people against an enemy whom he had no reason to hate. Ali's attitude was controversial, and many parts of society decided to make an example of him, including the government…

3½ YEARS

How long Ali was prevented from fighting by every state athletic commission. He lost out on some of his prime years as a boxer because of his political convictions.

ALI WAS FINED $10,000

Ali was taken to court by the US Department of Justice and found guilty in court of refusing induction into the US army. He was given a five-year prison sentence, although he remained free on bail.

KEEPING TABS

The Federal Bureau of Investigation (or FBI) carried out surveillance on Ali during the late 1960s because of his involvement with the Nation of Islam and his outspoken comments on the Vietnam War. The documents the FBI produced show the government agency believed that Ali's anti-war attitudes and support for civil rights could pose a 'subversive threat' to the country. Can you imagine being spied on by your government because of your beliefs?

WHAT'S THE FBI?

The US government's largest investigative agency, set up to investigate major crimes and oversee security issues that pose a threat to the country. Its director from 1924 to 1972 was the US official J Edgar Hoover, whose management of the agency was controversial. He was repeatedly accused of abusing the powers of the FBI to spy on and interfere with the lives of innocent civilians that he personally saw as a threat to the government because of their political activities.

DEPARTMENT OF JUSTICE
FEDERAL BUREAU OF INVESTIGATION
FIDELITY BRAVERY INTEGRITY

HIGHS & LOWS

Ali had been riding high before his unexpected break from boxing. When he returned, his skills had faded and he faced a long and bumpy road back to victory

Ali seemed to be unstoppable. He had wins against boxers including **George Chuvalo, Floyd Patterson, Ernie Terrell** and **Brian London.**

Fought and triumphed over **Cleveland Williams:**

100+
PUNCHES LANDED

4
KNOCKDOWNS

3
HIT ONLY 3 TIMES!

Ali makes his comeback and wins his first two fights against **Jerry Quarry** and **Oscar Bonavena.**

1965-1967

14 NOV, 1966

1970

JOE FRAZIER

8 MARCH, 1971

Ali vs Joe Frazier, the new heavyweight champion. For 14 rounds, the two boxers seemed evenly matched. Then, in the 15th, Frazier knocked Ali down with a left hook. Ali got back up, but Frazier was quickly declared the winner by all the judges. This was Ali's first defeat as a professional boxer.

CALLED 'THE FIGHT OF THE CENTURY'

GEORGE FOREMAN

10 CONSECUTIVE WINS

ALI'S CAREER RECORD: 56 WINS · 37 KOs · 5 LOSSES

WIN!

Ali bounced back with 10 victories in a row, but then he had his jaw broken by **Ken Norton**, in a fight that he lost. Ali bested Norton in a later rematch.

Ali goes head-to-head with the young champion **George Foreman** and wins back his heavyweight title after seven years (see 'Rumble in the Jungle').

Ali faces Frazier again in a non-title match and beats him.

He successfully defends his title in 10 fights, including one against Frazier (see 'Thrilla in Manila').

31 MARCH, 1973

30 OCT, 1974

1974

1975

OLYMPIC GOLD MEDALLIST LEON SPINKS HAD ONLY FOUGHT 7 PRO BOUTS WHEN HE BEAT ALI.

15 FEB, 1978

1979

Ali loses his title to **Leon Spinks** in a 15-round split decision. Seven months later, he defeats Spinks in a 15-round unanimous decision to reclaim the heavyweight title, becoming the first boxer to win it three times!

He announces his retirement from the sport. In 1980-81, Ali tries to launch a boxing comeback, but after losses to **Larry Holmes** and **Trevor Berbick**, he retires permanently.

LEON SPINKS

WIN! WIN! WIN!

3 TIMES WINNER OF THE WORLD HEAVYWEIGHT TITLE

WHEN? 30 OCTOBER, 1974

KINSHASA

ZAIRE
(Democratic Republic of the Congo)

WHERE?
The city of Kinshasa in Zaire (which is now the Democratic Republic of the Congo). Ali was treated like a hero by the people of Zaire when he arrived in their country because of his championing of the rights of Africans and Black Americans.

WHAT HAPPENED?
For pretty much the first time in his career, Ali was seen as the underdog. Foreman's youth, strength and massive size made him the favourite. But Ali had a smart strategy: he used his famous 'rope-a-dope' technique, leaning on the ring ropes and letting Foreman tire himself out while avoiding his heaviest blows. Once Foreman was flagging, Ali knocked him out in the eighth round and won back the title.

WHO ORGANISED IT?
The famous and controversial boxing promoter Don King. King's arrangement of the fight raised his profile and helped – along with his eccentric hairstyle and flair for the theatrical – to make him one of the most recognisable personalities in boxing for decades to come.

ZAIRE 74
This three-day music festival was organised by Don King as part of the promotion of the match and featured live performances from major R&B and soul artists, including James Brown and B B King.

RUMBLE IN THE JUNGLE

This epic showdown between Ali and the reigning heavyweight champion George Foreman shook the world and cemented Ali's return to the boxing bigtime

WATCHED BY
60%
GLOBAL POPULATION

1 BILLION TELEVISION VIEWERS!

GENERATED $100 MILLION IN REVENUE!

WHEN WE WERE KINGS

This documentary film about the fight released in 1996 was well-received and won the Academy Award for Best Documentary Feature.

'ROPE-A-DOPE'

Ali borrowed this strategy from boxing legend and former light-heavyweight champion Archie Moore, whom he had fought and beaten in 1962. Moore was popular with audiences and feared by other fighters.

GEORGE FOREMAN

BORN 1949, 1.92-METRES TALL
76 WINS, 68 KNOCKOUTS, 5 LOSSES

2X HEAVYWEIGHT CHAMPION OF THE WORLD IN 1973-1974 & 1994-1995

HEAVYWEIGHT BOXING GOLD MEDAL IN 1968 OLYMPIC GAMES IN MEXICO CITY

LEARNED TO BOX IN A US JOB CORPS CAMP: A PLACE WHERE POOR, AT-RISK YOUNG PEOPLE WERE GIVEN THE SKILLS AND ACADEMIC TRAINING REQUIRED IN THE WORKPLACE.

OLDEST EVER
HEAVYWEIGHT CHAMPION WHEN HE REGAINED THE TITLE IN 1994

WHEN?
1 OCTOBER, 1975

WHERE?
The Araneta Coliseum in Quezon City in the Philippines, southeast Asia. The ruthless dictator of the Philippines, Ferdinand Marcos, campaigned to host and sponsor the match to bring global attention to his country.

CAPITAL CITY OF THE PHILIPPINES SINCE

1948

QUEZON CITY

THE PHILIPPINES

BEST OF ENEMIES

There was no love lost between Ali and Frazier. Frazier was hurt by Ali's constant insults, while Ali resented the fact that Frazier was responsible for his first professional defeat. During a live broadcast before their second match, they exchanged heated words until Frazier stood up and challenged Ali and the two men had to be pulled apart by their entourages!

THRILLA IN MANILA

WATCHED BY 1 BILLION PEOPLE!

WHAT HAPPENED

Ali taunted Frazier verbally in the build-up to the fight and in the ring, to make his opponent mad and try to trick him into foolish mistakes. It didn't work.

Ali dominated in the early rounds, trying to score a knockout. By the fifth round, Frazier had found his feet and had Ali up against the ropes, delivering a relentless series of blows.

By round 12, Frazier had begun to tire and Ali regained the upper hand. In all, the two boxers went 14 gruelling rounds.

By the end, Frazier's right eye was swollen shut. Frazier's trainer, Eddie Futch, refused to let him go out for the 15th round, making Ali the victor.

14 ROUNDS

JOE FRAZIER

1944-2011. 1.8 METRES TALL

WORLD HEAVYWEIGHT BOXING CHAMPION FROM 1970 TO 1973, WHEN HE WAS BEATEN BY GEORGE FOREMAN IN JAMAICA

TAUGHT HIMSELF TO FIGHT WHILE GROWING UP ON A FARM

WON A GOLD MEDAL AT THE 1964 TOKYO OLYMPIC GAMES

AFTER HIS RETIREMENT, HE OPERATED A GYM IN PHILADELPHIA, US

The brutal bout between Ali and Joe Frazier in 1975 is often considered the greatest prize-fight of all time. What made it so special? And how bruising was it?

DEVASTATING DIAGNOSIS

In 1984, Ali was diagnosed with Parkinson's disease. It is possible that the condition was caused by the many blows to the head that he received during his time in boxing.

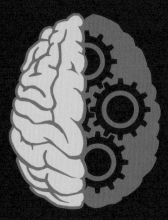

WHAT IS PARKINSON'S DISEASE?

An illness that causes progressive damage to some parts of the brain over time. The main symptoms are:

BODY TREMORS (uncontrollable shaking)	STIFF MUSCLES
SLOWER MOVEMENT	BALANCE PROBLEMS

Some people can find it difficult to carry out everyday activities on their own in the more advanced stages of the disease.

PEACE KEEPING

Despite his ailment, Ali travelled the world making appearances in aid of charities and humanitarian causes.

WHAT ALI DID NEXT...

After his boxing career was over, Ali searched for new ways to build his legacy and remain an inspirational force in the world. Sadly, his final years were also marked by serious illness...

1990

Ali meets Iraqi leader Saddam Hussein to help negotiate the release of American soldiers during the Gulf War.

2002

Ali travels to Afghanistan as a United Nations Messenger of Peace.

ALI'S TROPHY CABINET

'SPORTING PERSONALITY OF THE CENTURY'
BBC

SPORTS ILLUSTRATED
'SPORTSMAN OF THE CENTURY'

5x
'FIGHTER OF THE YEAR'
in Ring Magazine

2005

Awarded the Presidential Medal of Freedom in a 2005 ceremony at the White House by President George W Bush. It is the highest civilian award in the United States, given to people who've made great achievements in the arts, sports, sciences and the promotion of world peace.

President's Award from the NAACP (National Association for the Advancement of Colored People)

An inaugural inductee to the International Boxing Hall of Fame in 1990, set up to honour boxers, trainers and other people involved in the sport.

THE MUHAMMAD ALI CENTER

COST

$60 MILLION DOLLARS

This non-profit museum and cultural centre was founded by Ali in 2005. Located in his birthplace of Louisville, it features interactive exhibits, educational programming and special events designed to promote the importance of peace and social responsibility.

FAMILY MATTERS

Ali's daughter Laila Amaria Ali took up her father's profession and is widely considered one of the greatest female boxers of all time. She won super middleweight and light heavyweight titles and retired undefeated in 2007.

WIVES

CHILDREN

R.I.P.
After his death in 2016 from septic shock, the memorial service included a festival of public arts and educational events called 'I am Ali'.

20 MILE LONG

Funeral procession

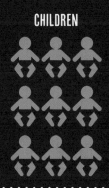

TYSON FURY (1988-)
NICKNAME: THE GYPSY KING
2.06 METRES TALL

MIKE TYSON (1966-)
NICKNAME: IRON MIKE
1.78 METRES TALL

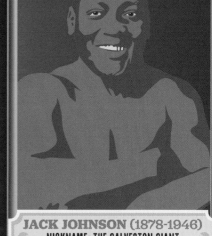

JACK JOHNSON (1878-1946)
NICKNAME: THE GALVESTON GIANT
1.84 METRES TALL

From an **Irish Traveller background**, Fury has overcome prejudice, depression and addiction outside of the ring to become the current World Boxing Council heavyweight champion, beating American fighter Deontay Wilder to claim the title in 2020. He is also known for his controversial remarks and attention-grabbing stunts, including dressing up as **Batman** in public!

Tyson learned to box while at a reform school, where he had been sent because of his childhood involvement with **street gangs**. Shorter than most professional boxers, his **speed** and **aggression** allowed him to dominate in the ring. He became the **youngest** ever heavyweight champion when he beat Trevor Berbick in 1986 in a second-round knockout.

Johnson was the **first Black American** heavyweight champion, winning the title by knocking out Tommy Burns in a 1908 match in Sydney, **Australia**. In his personal and professional lives, Johnson had to deal with racial prejudice, including widespread hostility from white Americans.

Muhammad Ali might be 'the greatest', but there are many other boxing legends from the sport's long history. Here are some other iconic fighters...

HEAVY

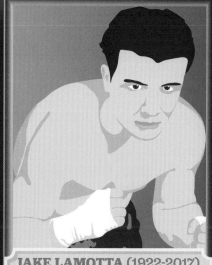

JAKE LAMOTTA (1922-2017)
NICKNAME: THE BRONX BULL
1.73 METRES TALL

SUGAR RAY ROBINSON (1921-1989)
NICKNAME: SUGAR, 1.8 METRES TALL

Turning to boxing as a career path while spending time in jail, the Italian American LaMotta was known for his strategy of letting an opponent wear themselves out giving him a beating, before turning on them and laying them out cold. He became middleweight champion in 1949. Later in life, he became an actor and a stand-up comedian. His life story was turned into the critically-acclaimed movie *Raging Bull* starring Robert DeNiro.

Another contender for the title of greatest boxer in history, Robinson was a six times world champion between 1946 and 1960 in both the welterweight and middleweight classes. He had 201 professional bouts and 109 knockouts, losing only 19 times.

'SUGAR'

6 TIMES WORLD CHAMPION

Raging Bull

HITTERS

GLOSSARY

Communist
Someone who believes in Communism, a social system where all property is owned by the entire community instead of individuals.

Degenerative
When a medical condition causes something to decline and break down over time.

Dictator
A ruler of a country who has total power over how it is run and its citizens.

Discrimination
Treating someone unfairly or differently because of their race, sex, age or disability.

Drafted
When someone is selected for recruitment into the army, whether they want to join or not.

Equality
The belief that everyone should have the same rights and opportunities.

Humanitarian
Activities designed to promote the wellbeing of human populations in deprived parts of the world.

Leverage
Using something to exert more force on something else, such as using the ropes in a boxing ring to put more force into your punches during a bout.

Nationalist
Someone who campaigns for the independence of a particular nation or people.

Orthodox
The traditional and mainstream beliefs of a particular religion.

First published 2024 by Button Books, an imprint of Guild of Master Craftsman Publications Ltd, Castle Place, 166 High Street, Lewes, East Sussex, BN7 1XU, UK. Copyright in the Work © GMC Publications Ltd, 2024. ISBN 978 1 78708 147 5. Distributed by Publishers Group West in the United States. All rights reserved. No part of this publication may be reproduced, stored in a retrieval system, or transmitted in any form or by any means without the prior permission of the publisher and copyright owner. While every effort has been made to obtain permission from the copyright holders for all material used in this book, the publishers will be pleased to hear from anyone who has not been appropriately acknowledged and to make the correction in future reprints. The publishers and authors can accept no legal responsibility for any consequences arising from the application of information, advice, or instructions given in this publication. A catalogue record for this book is available from the British Library. Senior Project Editor: Nick Pierce. Design: Tim Lambert, Dean Chillmaid. Illustrations: Alex Bailey, Ben Bissett, Matt Carr, Shutterstock. Colour origination by GMC Reprographics. Printed and bound in China.